THINKING ~~OF~~
PERFORMI~~NG?~~

**There are thousan~~ds~~ ~~of plays and music~~als
available to perform fro~~m ~~so ~~mu~~ch right
now, and applying for ~~a licenc~~e is easier and
more affordable ~~th~~an you might think**

From classic plays to brand new musicals, from monologues
to epic dramas, there are shows for everyone.

Plays and musicals are protected by copyright law, so if you
want to perform them, the first thing you'll need is a licence.
This simple process helps support the playwright by ensuring
they get paid for their work and means that you'll have the
documents you need to stage the show in public.

Not all our shows are available to perform all the time, so it's
important to check and apply for a licence before you start
rehearsals or commit to doing the show.

LEARN MORE &
FIND THOUSANDS OF SHOWS

Browse our full range of plays and musicals, and find out
more about how to license a show
www.samuelfrench.co.uk/perform

Talk to the friendly experts in our Licensing team for advice
on choosing a show and help with licensing
plays@samuelfrench.co.uk   020 7387 9373

Acting Editions

BORN TO PERFORM

Playscripts designed from the ground up to work the way you do in rehearsal, performance and study

---

Larger, clearer text for easier reading

Wider margins for notes

Performance features such as character and props lists, sound and lighting cues, and more

---

+ CHOOSE A SIZE AND STYLE TO SUIT YOU

STANDARD EDITION

Our regular paperback book at our regular size

SPIRAL-BOUND EDITION

The same size as the Standard Edition, but with a sturdy, easy-to-fold, easy-to-hold spiral-bound spine

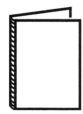

LARGE EDITION

A4 size and spiral bound, with larger text and a blank page for notes opposite every page of text – perfect for technical and directing use

---

LEARN MORE | **samuelfrench.co.uk/actingeditions**

CACOPHONY

by Molly Taylor

‖SAMUEL FRENCH‖

samuelfrench.co.uk

Other plays by MOLLY TAYLOR
published and licensed by Samuel French

Extinguished Things

FIND PERFECT PLAYS TO PERFORM AT
www.samuelfrench.co.uk/perform

MUSIC USE NOTE

Licensees are solely responsible for obtaining formal written permission from copyright owners to use copyrighted music in the performance of this play and are strongly cautioned to do so. If no such permission is obtained by the licensee, then the licensee must use only original music that the licensee owns and controls. Licensees are solely responsible and liable for all music clearances and shall indemnify the copyright owners of the play(s) and their licensing agent, Samuel French, against any costs, expenses, losses and liabilities arising from the use of music by licensees. Please contact the appropriate music licensing authority in your territory for the rights to any incidental music.

IMPORTANT BILLING AND CREDIT REQUIREMENTS

If you have obtained performance rights to this title, please refer to your licensing agreement for important billing and credit requirements.

ALMEIDA
THEATRE

The Almeida Theatre makes brave new work that asks big questions: of plays, of theatre and of the world around us.

Whether new work or reinvigorated classics, the Almeida brings together the most exciting artists to take risks; to provoke, inspire and surprise our audiences.

Recent highlights include Rupert Goold's Olivier Award-winning production of *Ink* (transferred to the West End and transfers to Broadway in 2019), Robert Icke's productions of *Hamlet* (transferred to the West End and was broadcast on BBC TWO), *Mary Stuart* (transferred to the West End and toured the UK) and *The Wild Duck*, and Rebecca Frecknall's production of *Summer and Smoke* (transferred to the West End).

Other notable productions have included *American Psycho: a new musical thriller* (transferred to Broadway); *Chimerica* (won three Olivier Awards and transferred to the West End); *King Charles III* (won the Olivier Award for Best New Play and transferred to the West End and Broadway, toured the UK and Sydney, and was adapted into a BAFTA-nominated TV drama); and *Oresteia* (transferred to the West End and won the Olivier Award for Best Director).

Matthew Needham and Patsy Ferran in *Summer and Smoke* by Tennessee Williams, directed by Rebecca Frecknall at the Almeida Theatre (2018)
Photo by Marc Brenner

almeida.co.uk
🐦 @AlmeidaTheatre
📘 /almeidatheatre
📷 @almeida_theatre

Artistic Director **Rupert Goold**

Executive Director **Denise Wood**

Associate Directors **Robert Icke, Rebecca Frecknall**

Registered Charity no. 282167

 Supported using public funding by
**ARTS COUNCIL
ENGLAND**

Principal Partner

ASPEN

ALMEIDA PARTICIPATION

Our Participation programme inspires and engages young people and our local community, giving them opportunities to create theatre with the most exciting artists working in the industry today. Those participating in our projects are in a two-way dialogue with us, learning from directors, actors, writers and producers, and also influencing and shaping our work in the future.

MORE INFORMATION

@ATParticipate
facebook.com/almeida.participate
almeida.co.uk/participation
020 7288 4916
participate@almeida.co.uk

Director of Participation and Work for Young People **Dani Parr**
Participation Producer **Ross Crosby**
Participation Associate: Schools **Jo Carey**
Participation Associate: Young Artists **Mike Bryher**
Participation Administrator **Sarah Stallwood-Hall**
Participation Intern **Valerie Sadoh**

Almeida Participation is incredibly grateful to all our supporters, Trusts and Foundations, individuals and companies who have supported our work in 2017/18.

ABOUT THE AUTHOR

Molly Taylor is a playwright and theatre-maker, based in London.

She began making work when she was an Associate of the National Theatre of Scotland. Her first production, *Love Letters to the Public Transport System*, toured Scotland in 2012 and won the Critics' Circle Award, Adelaide Fringe 2018. Her most recent production, *Extinguished Things*, had a sell-out run at the Edinburgh Fringe Festival 2018, and won the Holden Street Theatre Award.

She works extensively in the participatory sector, making work with professional and non-professional performers. Recently she has made work for the Bush Theatre, the Young Vic, and VAULT Festival. She is currently working on projects with The BRIT School and The Yard.

AUTHOR'S NOTE

The play is set in the present day.

The world of the play exists in a liminal 'nowhere' space, where characters are trying to piece their memories together. Their versions of past events spring into life. Sometimes the liminal world and memories / reconstructions blur into one another.

The space should therefore have an ethereal quality, with minimal props, and avoid aiming for naturalism.

The staging is flexible; the original production was staged in the round, with cast members seated amongst the audience at the top of the show. The 2019 production was staged end-on.

Multi-role playing of smaller parts is advised, but those characters closest to Abi (friends, family & Seb) should be played by actors that don't multi-role. The character of Tash is present through most of the play, directly involved or silently observing, so it's key that the actor doesn't play more than one part.

A slash in the text (/) indicates overlapping dialogue. A dash (–) indicates interruption.

CREATIVE LIST

MICHAEL BRYHER

Michael Bryher is a theatre-maker, director and facilitator. He trained at LAMDA and has worked as an actor for companies including Kneehigh, The RSC, and dreamthinkspeak. In 2013 he was a finalist for the JMK award. He also runs Dumbshow, and over the last seven years has toured his work nationally and internationally. He has recently edited a volume of audition monologues for young people for Nick Hern Books, and created the Christmas show for the Nuffield Theatre Southampton in 2018.

KHADIJA RAZA

Khadija Raza studied BA Design for Stage at the Royal Central School of Speech and Drama and was winner of the Linbury Prize 2017 for the Unicorn Theatre, and Stage Debut Award for best designer, 2018. Previous credits include; as designer: *Elephant in the Room* – R&D (Camden People's Theatre), *Cacophony* and *Loki & Cassie: A Love Story* (Almeida Theatre Young Company), *Spun* (Arcola Theatre), *No One Is Coming To Save You* (Bunker Theatre and Edinbrugh Fringe), *MIXTAPE* (Royal Exchange Theatre), *Hijabi Monologues* (Bush Theatre), *I Want You To Admire Me/But You Shouldn't* (Camden People's Theatre), *From Morning to Midnight* (Webber Douglas Studio) and as assistant: *The Unknown Island* (Gate Theatre), *L'heure Espagnole* and *Gianni Schicci* (Opera Nationale de Lorraine).

GERMMA ORLEANS-THOMPSON

Germma Orleans-Thompson is a theatre-maker and producer. She graduated from the Drama and Theatre Studies BA at the University of Kent in 2017 and moved to London two months later to become the Participation Intern at the Almeida Theatre from 2017-2018. As a freelance producer, she has worked on *You Must Learn To Understand* (Almeida Theatre, Battersea Arts Centre). She is the co-founder of Sculptress Theatre Company, a duo who break boundaries by creating work that is not judged by the colour of their skin, but by the content of their hearts. Sculptress Theatre is a Creative Talent company, funded by Creative Youth.

ACKNOWLEDGEMENTS

This play was developed live in rehearsals with the members of the 2017/18 Almeida Young Company (19-25); it benefitted from a collective consciousness, with countless important perspectives. Thanks to the original actors for being vigorous and generous, and pointing me in the right direction when I was missing a trick.

Thanks too to Almeida Participation; Dani Parr, Ross Crosby, and Germma Orleans-Thompson, for putting your support and weight behind this production.

We're extremely grateful to Jon Ronson, whose book *So You've Been Publicly Shamed* acted as our starting point, and gave us such huge scope for research. Thanks for giving us an insight into your process and storytelling.

The most gratitude goes to Michael Bryher, who not only developed the story, but whose fearless direction made this piece suddenly click into something more than the sum of its parts. He chipped and chiselled away at this play until it worked, and it made me a better writer. Thank you Mike.

FIRST PERFORMANCE

Cacophony was first performed at the Almeida Theatre
26-28 July 2018 with the following cast:

Abi – **Annie Hawkins**
Cookie – **Tiwalade Ibirogba Olulode**
Tash – **Helena Morais**
Tolu – **Eddie Boyce-Rodgers**
Tobias – **Ben Quashie**
Will – **Corey Peterson**
Daisy – **Charlie Dylan**
Rosa – **Hannah Donelon**
Joanna – **Lucy Shafi**
Seb – **David Bankole**
March Organiser 1 – **Ashley Rose**
Iggy/Reluctant Friend/Headteacher/Paparazzi – **Tim Dennett**
Stacey/Enthusiastic Protestor/Bystander
– **Lauren McGarvey**
Publicist/March Organiser 2 – **Khanyiso Mtwana**
March Organiser 3/Fan – **Lao Lee**
Rum and Coke/Volunteer/Radio Presenter
– **Simeon Blake-Hall**
Journalist/Father – **Samson Cox-Vinell**

CREATIVE TEAM

Story developed by Molly Taylor and Michael Bryher
Created with the Almeida Young Company

Writer – Molly Taylor
Director – Michael Bryher
Designer – Khadija Raza
Sound Designer – George Lumkin
Lighting Designer – Katie Nicoll
Movement Direction – Edd Mitton
Assistant Director – Germma Orleans-Thompson
Producer – Ross Crosby

Cacophony opened at The Yard Theatre on
19th February–22 February 2019 with the following cast:

Abi – **Annie Hawkins**
Cookie – **Tiwalade Ibirogba Oluode**
Tash – **Helena Morais**
Tolu – **Sonny Poon Tip**
Tobias – **Ben Quashie**
Will – **Azan Ahmed**
Daisy – **Charlie Dylan**
Rosa – **Lauren McGarvery**
Joanna – **Lucy Shafi**
Seb – **David Bankole**
March Organiser 1 – **Ashley Rose**
Iggy/Reluctant Friend/Headteacher/Paparazzi – **Tim Dennett**
Stacey/Mother/Bystander – **Bridget Rudder**
March Organiser 2/Fan – **Caroline Elms**
March Organiser 3/Publicist – **Sasha Venmore Rowland**
Rum and Coke/Volunteer/Radio Presenter – **James Bullen**
Journalist/Enthusiastic Protestor – **Adam Hasyim Cranfield**

To Sam, with love.

CHARACTERS

ABI – A woman in her early 20s

COOKIE
TASH
TOLU
TOBIAS } Abi's friends and flatmates
WILL
STACEY
IGGY

SEB – Abi's boyfriend

JOANNA
DAISY } Abi's siblings

MO 1
MO 2 } March organisers
MO 3

ROSA – A woman in her 30s

PUBLICIST
PAPARAZZI
JOURNALIST
RADIO PRESENTER
HEADTEACHER
BYSTANDER
FAN
VOLUNTEER
RUM AND COKE
FATHER

Scene One – Where did it begin?

The cast are sat amongst the audience, in the round.
The floor is a shiny reflective black, an oil slick that
has cleared everything in its path. The space is empty,
a hollow gap where **ABI** *should be.*

COOKIE *enters the space, and places a chair centre stage.*
TASH *joins her.*

TASH I need you to take me through it. How did it happen...
can we go back? When was the last time you saw her?

Everyone is trying to identify when, but no one answers.

COOKIE She was wearing that blue oversized hoodie she used
to wear.

TOLU With the coffee stain on the sleeve.

COOKIE Yeah. She was coming out of the flat.

TOBIAS No, that was a photo.

COOKIE Was it?

TOBIAS Yeah.

TOLU She's looking at the camera, with her hair scraped back.

TASH I've seen that photo in the paper.

TOLU She's on her own.

TASH Yeah.

JOANNA She looked tired.

DAISY She'd been round to see us, hadn't she?

JOANNA Yeah.

SEB She was standing in my bedroom. Not saying anything.

TASH But when did it start?

Beat.

COOKIE I reckon it started back when we were about thirteen or fourteen. PSHE. Remember?

Cast members sweep into the space and recreate the school scene with their chairs. **ABI***'s remains empty.*

We had been campaigning to get rid of the school skirts, protesting for weeks, rolling them up round our arses to make a point.

ROSA*, on a chair, twigs.*

ROSA Hang on, this was all a long time before I ever met Abi. So I shouldn't be here.

She leaves the space.

COOKIE Abi's parents had a printer, remember Tash, and we went round to hers to print out the posters?

TASH Yeah. But that's too far back.

Chairs are cleared by actors who go back to their positions amongst the audience.

SEB *is alone with the empty chair.*

SEB For me it was the second night we spent together. She was tired and restless and all of a sudden she asked if she could use my laptop and started typing away. I watched her.

TASH At what point?

SEB That was the day after.

MO 1 Oh right, well we weren't about yet.

JOURNALIST	RADIO PRESENTER	PAPARAZZI
Me neither.	I hadn't met her yet.	Nah.

JOANNA *and* DAISY *suddenly in the space.*

JOANNA For us it started a long time before any of this. When we were kids.

DAISY Yeah, she used to play hide and seek with me, but she was too good at hiding.

JOANNA Yeah you used to come in crying, saying you'd lost her.

TASH *trying to make sense.*

TASH Yeah – but. I can't. Can we go back to the BBQ? That's the last thing I remember.

DAISY We weren't there, were we?

DAISY *and* JOANNA *gone.*

TOLU, WILL, TOBIAS, STACEY, COOKIE, IGGY *in the space.*

TASH It was Tolu's birthday.

TOLU Guys, this is Stacey.

STACEY Am I going out with you at this point?

TOLU Yeah.

TOBIAS You weren't sitting there.

IGGY No, Abi was sitting there.

The chair becomes empty, waiting for her.

COOKIE *(to* TOBIAS*)* You were upstairs.

TOBIAS Was I?

TOBIAS *out of the space.*

WILL Anyone thought about offering me a drink?

TOLU You live here mate, you can get your own.

WILL Fine.

TASH Yes. Yes, I remember this.

ABI *somehow in the in-between space, they are back to where it all began.*

(to **ABI***)* Abi, is this going to be OK?

ABI What do you mean?

TASH It's just. It's good to see you.

ABI Why are you being weird?

Scene Two – BBQ party

The garden of ABI*'s flat, a BBQ to celebrate* TOLU*'s birthday. Music coming from the kitchen, a stream of people who enter, drink, go back into the house. Friday night crackle. Shit bottled beers. People talking over each other and zoning into other conversations. Some of the party are well acquainted, some less so.* TOLU *is looking after his new girlfriend.*

COOKIE He's been acquitted.

TASH Has he??

ABI Yeah.

TASH You are kidding.

WILL Who?

ABI Mark Rendell – that QPR player.

WILL What you talking about?

COOKIE The rape trial?

TASH Got no respect for a system that is entirely rigged against listening to women.

WILL I hear you sista!

TASH Why should we have any respect for justice when – sorry – are you taking the piss?

WILL Yeah.

ABI Seven men on the jury. Just saying.

COOKIE You've got to name that shit. Name it.

TASH God this is so depressing *(checking the story on her phone).*

IGGY *enters.*

IGGY Does anyone want anything for tonight? I'm gonna call him now.

ABI Ah yeah maybe.

COOKIE No thanks.

TOLU *(to* **IGGY***)* Yes mate.

WILL Is it a proper night?

ABI Might be.

WILL Come on then!

> **IGGY** *on the phone.*

> **TOLU** *introducing* **STACEY***.*

TOLU Guys, this is Stacey – Stacey – everyone.

> *They greet her hello.*

COOKIE Hey.

STACEY No, hi, yeah, nice flat, cute garden, it's sweet.

COOKIE I don't actually live here – these guys do –

TOLU She squats.

STACEY Do you for real?

TOLU No.

COOKIE I'm just waiting for Tobias to move out. Then I'm in.

TOLU Can we make that happen?

WILL Here you go darling.

TASH *(consulting her phone)* So the march outside the court tomorrow –

ABI Yeah.

TASH Are we all up for it?

COOKIE Definitely. Walk the hangover off.

TASH Nice one.

TOLU Stacey's just about to go hiking in Kilimanjaro, aren't you Stace?

STACEY Yeah. A charity thing.

TASH That's cool.

ABI Hey – was it your interview this morning?

TASH Yeah. Went well.

COOKIE Yeah?

TASH I have a horrible feeling they are going to offer it to me. I was hearing myself answering the questions and I was like – why are you being so enthusiastic?

COOKIE It's hard in an interview though.

TASH Hopefully they saw through it.

ABI Fingers crossed.

WILL Just do it for a bit and then leave.

TASH I can't be arsed, I want a straight no.

    TOBIAS *enters, a bit flustered.*

TOBIAS Who's responsible for the girl on my bed?

COOKIE Who is it?

TOBIAS Not a clue.

IGGY *(faux shock-horror)* Shit! Did she get past the sign?

TOBIAS Yeah.

ABI What sign?

TOBIAS 'DO NOT ENTER'.

ABI Jokes.

TOBIAS Anyone she belong to?

ABI No idea who she is.

TOBIAS Fuck's sake.

WILL What she look like?

TOBIAS Dunno, she's face down. Blue hair at the ends.

IGGY Ah. Cheyanne. That's Cheyanne.

TOBIAS Well do you want to get her off my bed?

IGGY Not particularly.

TOLU She's just having a disco nap, leave her.

TOBIAS I did say, guys, I did say if we were having a party then I wanted my room out-of-bounds.

TOLU You did say that, you did. He said that, didn't he?

ABI He did. You did say that, Tobes.

TOLU We'll all be out of here soon anyway, so just leave her for now.

ABI We'll get rid of her when we go.

COOKIE What's up with her?

TOBIAS She's wrecked.

COOKIE Shame.

TOBIAS I really don't want some stranger conked out on my bed, OK? If I'm going to go to bed.

WILL You wouldn't be strangers then though, would you?

ABI You not coming out, Tobes?

TOBIAS Dunno.

ABI You are! You have to come out.

TOLU It's my birthday!

ABI It's his birthday!

TOBIAS I know, I'm celebrating it now, aren't I?

ABI Are you?? Come on, come and sit here and have a drink with us.

STACEY I can go and check if you like.

TOLU She'll be fine.

STACEY I'm quite good with drunk people. I can get through to them.

IGGY You're actually *not allowed* to enter his room, Stacey.

TOLU True.

> **TOBIAS** *goes back to deal with the problem.* **TASH** *still consulting her phone.*

TASH Have you read all these WhatsApp messages from Mark Rendell's phone?

COOKIE From the trial?

TASH Unbelievable.

ABI What do they say?

TASH Read. *(Hands her phone over)*

COOKIE That he can be acquitted with that evidence.

IGGY What messages?

TASH Vile and quite incriminating stuff about the girl, that he sent the following day.

WILL Is it?

COOKIE They're disgusting.

> **IGGY**, **WILL** *and* **STACEY** *intermittently look, along with* **ABI**.

STACEY That doesn't mean he raped her.

COOKIE Have you read them?

TASH It looks very much like Mark Rendell is a rapist.

TOLU So what's the plan then, guys? Is your guy coming here?

IGGY Yeah.

COOKIE If you stack up that evidence then you've got a really compelling case for a man who is using his power to sexually subordinate women.

STACEY Or you've got some guy with shit WhatsApp banter.

WILL Don't get me wrong – he does sound like a dick.

STACEY Being a dick doesn't make him a rapist.

WILL Exactly.

ABI Yeah but –

WILL But, like, beyond reasonable doubt. There is reasonable
doubt. Does he deserve a jail sentence?

COOKIE He deserves a lobotomy.

TASH Is the plan to meet at the court then, what time?

ABI Ten? Half ten?

STACEY If he's been acquitted, what's the march for?

COOKIE It's for us, Stacey, it's for us.

STACEY Are you personally invested?

COOKIE What?

STACEY No, I'm just asking.

COOKIE Yes, I'm definitely 'personally invested'.

STACEY Oh OK.

COOKIE Some dickhead footballer with all that money and all
that power and everything that comes with it –

WILL He plays for QPR!

COOKIE Oh right!

ABI What has that got to do with it?

TASH He's only a lower league rapist, Abi.

ABI Oh. Right. Fine then.

WILL He's not a rapist!

COOKIE His whole career is about being held up as an
untouchable thing – untouchable.

WILL He's been acquitted!

COOKIE That's not the point!

WILL Jury of public opinion, is it?

TOLU Anyone need anything?

STACEY I'm not quite sure what the point is, to be honest.

TOLU Top up? Anyone?

TASH Just because he's been acquitted doesn't mean it ceases to be an issue, and you shouldn't be so fixated on the acquittal because the system in the first instance is at fault.

WILL I'm not fixated on it, it's just a fact.

COOKIE Do you have complete trust in the court system?

  STACEY *gets up and wanders inside.*

TOLU Guys, not being funny, I'm all up for debate but it's my birthday –

ABI *(to* **IGGY***)* Did you get the –

IGGY All done, on its way.

TOLU And I'm trying to get laid here so...less rapey maybe?

WILL It won't happen for you tonight, mate.

TOLU What?

WILL It's jam sandwich time.

ABI Will!

WILL I can smell it.

TOLU You're fucking disgusting.

  TOBIAS *enters, fuming.*

TOBIAS She's been sick next to my bin.

IGGY Shit.

TOBIAS Not *in* my bin. Right next to my bin. Still passed out.

COOKIE Look, we'll help clean up.

TOLU Not now we won't, we need to be making a move –

ABI Take her up some water. Look, I'll come up.

>   **ABI** *and* **TOBIAS** *exit.*

>   **IGGY** *has been studying the phone and the WhatsApp messages.*

IGGY Some women like to be degraded.

>   *Pause.*

COOKIE What?

IGGY I'm not saying he's innocent, I'm just saying.

STACEY Well if they want to be degraded then that's fine, but don't go round the next day saying you've been raped.

WILL The point is, there wasn't enough proof to convict.

TOLU Are we getting the bus or an Uber?

IGGY Saying that, I think he did it.

WILL They sent WhatsApp messages and that does not make them rapists –

TOLU Guys are we getting an Uber or what?

WILL That's what the court is there for.

TOLU *(to himself)* Yes, Uber, thanks Tolu.

>   **ABI** *and* **STACEY** *re-enter.*

ABI Cheyanne is out of it.

COOKIE But the court is failing these women.

TASH Look, I know it's complicated –

WILL It's over.

TASH But –

COOKIE It is to you.

WILL No, it just is, Cookie!

STACEY I don't know enough about the trial, to be honest –

TOLU Can we just –

ABI I can believe that what he thought was consensual wasn't.

TASH Yes, and that's what's scary.

COOKIE That doesn't make him innocent!

WILL I'm just saying –

COOKIE Go on, what?

WILL I'm just saying that those –

COOKIE Say it.

WILL I'm going to, I'm just –

COOKIE Say it, you've got the floor – say it. I'm intrigued.

WILL I'm trying!

STACEY Shut up, Cookie, let him speak.

WILL There's so many people jumping on the bandwagon because it's topical.

COOKIE It's not topical, Will, it's the opposite of topical! It's fucking old, mate, it's ancient.

TOLU Uber is four minutes away –

STACEY Did you just get the one? We need two.

COOKIE It's not a fucking bandwagon.

TOLU Anyone got Uber on their phone?

ABI I have.

TOLU Drink up, everyone!

TASH The point is, Will, just listen – what is happening when a man can rape a woman and he doesn't realise he's raping her?

WILL He didn't!

COOKIE Fuck's sake.

WILL Listen, listen yeah – sorry but – going back to your interview, yeah. All the signs are there that you want it, but you're claiming you don't want it – even though that's not what you're saying to them. Am I right though? Am I right? Can you see this, yeah?

He has scored a goal.

ABI Fuck off, Will.

TOBIAS *returns.*

TOBIAS No moving her.

IGGY What?

TOBIAS No. Tried shaking her.

COOKIE Don't.

TOBIAS She's paralytic –

COOKIE Doesn't matter, don't touch her.

ABI Guys, that's the other Uber booked.

TOLU Who is coming in the first one?

STACEY Me.

IGGY Me too.

WILL She's on his bed, how is he supposed to not touch her??

ABI Cookie, get your stuff –

WILL He's just trying to wake her up!

COOKIE I know what he's trying to do, I'm just giving him some advice!

TOLU *(to* **TASH***)* Are you coming with us?

TASH I might give it a miss, you know.

ABI No, you have to come!

TOLU I'm calling time! It's here, come on!

COOKIE I'm coming. *(To* **TASH***)* You staying?

TASH Yeah.

ABI You sure?

TASH Yeah, I'm knackered.

TOLU Move people!

ABI But I'll see you tomorrow? At the march.

TASH Definitely.

ABI OK, good, love you.

COOKIE Meet you outside the court?

TASH Yeah.

COOKIE Half ten. Don't be late.

TASH It's not me that's going out!

ABI *(to* **TASH***)* Don't clean up the sick.

They say goodbyes speedily and exit.

Scene Three – Night out

The world of the previous scene blends into this; the people at the BBQ become bodies on a dancefloor and it morphs directly into the world of the club night, like everyone in the place has the same pulse.

The DJ booth is unseen, but every so often avid dancers direct their energy to it, as if conversing silently with the DJ, fully-focused.

Someone passes a bottle of water to a mate, that person takes it, opens it, swigs it, and pours a bit over their head. Their friend wipes the water off their face, laughing.

Someone is properly fucked – or in a trance; stood, barely half-bouncing to the beat, feet planted. They stay upright, every so often pumping their fist in time to the music for a moment. As solid as a totem.

Someone asks a friend 'You feeling anything yet?'

Someone arrives with their hands straining around three or four rum and cokes, thrilled by their own offering – as if bringing a birthday cake to a table, as if they are the saviour of the party. Majestic. No one has ordered rum and coke. Someone takes one off him to be polite. Other people wave him away. He offers one to a passing girl he doesn't know – **ABI** *– who takes it.*

ABI For me?

RUM AND COKE Why not?

ABI Cheers! *(They clink glasses, she drinks, winces)*

He celebrates as if he's just crossed a finish line.

RUM AND COKE What's your name?

ABI Abi.

RUM AND COKE Amy?

ABI Abi!

RUM AND COKE I can't hear you!

ABI Who cares? Thanks for the drink *(she holds it aloft)*

RUM AND COKE What?

ABI The drink?

RUM AND COKE *(gesturing to his own)* No, I've got one!

She gives him a thumbs up. She's ready to move on. He's not. He's found a friend.

Someone is hugging their friend and saying 'I think you're probably the most amazing person in my life, no honestly, every day at work I just think I wish I could do what you do.'

A beat drops, the crowd roar. The DJ gets a lot of love.

Someone is instructing a friend 'Just keep an eye on her tonight, she normally doesn't take stuff.' The friend is nodding vigorously and going 'Yeah yeah yeah yeah yeah, I've got my eyes on her yeah.' S/he then goes to the person in question and says 'You OK, yeah, you're OK, come here' and embraces them.

RUM AND COKE *is dancing to where* **ABI** *is, like she is the north star.*

A friend to **ABI** *'I'm fucked, I think I'm gonna go home.'* **ABI** *pleads 'noooooooooo!'*

Bottles of water pass between people. Random acts of kindness. Glowsticks.

Someone is putting glitter on someone's face.

Someone's rucksack isn't zipped up properly.

Someone fucking loves this track.

Someone has lost an earring. Everyone is involved. People scouring the floor, addicted to helping, eyes everywhere 'What are we looking for??'

RUM AND COKE *is trying to engage* **ABI** *in more shit chat. She is polite. He tries to grab her hands as if to dance with her, but it looks so out of place. She's embarrassed for him.*

His friend – **SEB** *– has been watching.* **ABI** *wriggles away from* **RUM AND COKE**.

SEB You OK?

ABI Yeah.

SEB He bothering you?

ABI Bit intense.

SEB He's harmless. Clueless.

> **RUM AND COKE** *trying to dance to where they are,* **SEB** *mimes throwing a bone to a dog – there, there boy, fetch! As if to say – you've had a go now piss off.* **RUM AND COKE** *gives him the finger, but friendly.*

RUM AND COKE You wankerrrrrrr.

SEB I fucking love you mate.

RUM AND COKE I love your fucking...mum.

> *He reacts as if this is the finest punchline ever, a blaze of glory. He gestures to* **SEB**, *but talks to* **ABI**.

He's got crabs.

SEB I have.

ABI S'OK, I'm a cancer. I like crabs.

RUM AND COKE *(to* **SEB***)* She's got fucking cancer man.

RUM AND COKE *hugs* **ABI** *as if she's terminally ill, a dying Madonna.*

You're so fucking brave.

SEB Go and get me a drink.

RUM AND COKE *gestures 'drinks for everyone.'*

SEB *and* **ABI** *dance, gaze, dance, gaze. Giggle at nothing. Magnets.*

The space glows.

COOKIE *is leaving, grabs* **ABI** *to kiss goodbye.*

COOKIE Tomorrow? You know where?

ABI Yeah. Or send me a pin.

COOKIE Outside the courts.

ABI Yeah.

COOKIE Love you.

ABI Message me when you get in.

COOKIE I won't.

ABI Love you.

Sparkling space. Hands in the air. Tune vibrates. The crest of any night, the best night, the night when you could fall in love at a pin drop.

Someone tells someone their hair is fucking beautiful.

SEB You smoke?

ABI No. Do you?

SEB No.

ABI You want to go outside?

SEB Yeah.

Someone shouts – 'Fucking epic night'.

ABI I like your face.

SEB My face?

ABI Yeah. You've got a good face.

SEB Moisturising, innit. Nivea. Thank you.

ABI You're welcome.

SEB Yours isn't too bad either.

ABI Yeah?

SEB Yeah.

> **SEB** *touches her face as the crowd swells, she closes her eyes.*
>
> *Someone crashes into their moment, literally, danced off their feet.*
>
> *Someone, pumped, gurns at* **ABI** *and* **SEB**, *they laugh in sync.* **SEB** *takes* **ABI***'s hand and weaves her through the crowd.* **TOBIAS** *clocks them and grabs her other hand.*

TOBIAS You OK?

ABI Yeah!

TOBIAS You going?

ABI No! Just getting some fresh are. With... *(To* **SEB***)* I don't know your name.

SEB I don't know yours.

ABI Right then. With him.

TOBIAS OK, but don't say bye without bye, yeah?

ABI No, don't worry.

SEB I'm Seb.

ABI Abi.

SEB You look like an Abi.

ABI What does that look like?

SEB Lovely.

ABI What was your name again?

SEB Seb.

> *The music builds. Hands in the air to grasp the sounds.*
> *Like light through veins.* **RUM AND COKE** *is lifting an*
> *unsuspecting girl, lifting her like a prize. Music roars*
> *and builds to a climax – time jumps forward, an hour*
> *or two, bodies, including* **ABI** *and* **SEB** *thrust into the*
> *same pumping dance beat. One throng of limbs. Someone*
> *waves their T-shirt in the air. The space dances, intensely*
> *focused.* **ABI** *and* **SEB** *with their eyes on one another.*
> *Like the end of a fireworks display, everything bursting*
> *and everything light.*

Scene Four – One-night stand

The space obliterates – we're no longer in the club. It's quiet and softer. SEB *on his own.*

SEB I remember her forgetting my name throughout the night so I had to keep reminding her. Early morning, sun coming up. I'm getting called.

ABI Kevin.

SEB And.

ABI Freddie.

SEB And.

ABI Jack.

SEB She's a piss-taker. There's light creeping in through the curtains and there's a cereal bowl spot-lit, been there for days, crusty and shit – has she noticed? – Shoulda cleaned. The record player aching for a tune, her fingers thumbing through the vinyl, like she's introducing herself to every single record. I've never found fingers attractive before. She's making my room beautiful. Is she staying? Is she sleeping? Is it too late for me to get rid of that cereal bowl? Yes. Fuck it. Work. It's 8am or 9am and I need to be moving towards the door. She should sleep longer. Sleep. She looks good in my sheets.

I've got to go. You sleep.

ABI Fuck, what time is it?

Scene Five – Protest gathers

Protesters at the start point of the march, as people gather. Banners being unfurled. Chatter. **TASH, COOKIE, TOBIAS,** *and a few others gather. Protest organisers talking on radios. A few stewards in hi-vis.* **TOBIAS** *handing out coffees.*

COOKIE Did you get lost?

TOBIAS Sorry. It is rammed back there.

COOKIE Yeah, it's busy.

TASH Good turnout.

TOBIAS Soya?

TASH For me?

TOBIAS Who ordered soya?

COOKIE Not me.

TASH So did Abi go back to his then?

COOKIE Think so.

TOBIAS Did I order soya for myself?

TASH Shall I give her a call?

COOKIE Maybe she's gonna give it a miss.

TOBIAS Hate soya.

TASH Oh no – that's her – she says sorry, she's on her way.

COOKIE OK.

TASH I'll wait for her if you guys wanna head.

COOKIE No we can wait.

TOBIAS I'm playing fives at two.

TASH Go on, you go, s'fine.

COOKIE OK.

TASH Hang on – march selfie!

They pose.

Scene Six – Abi on her way to the march

ROSA *steps into the space where the march has been gathering, and splinters the memory.* TASH *sees her.*

TASH Is this when you and Abi met?

ROSA Yes, I was at the station.

The marchers begin to scatter.

Yeah.

TASH Weren't you pregnant at this point?

ROSA Yeah I was.

Hello you.

Slowly she begins to recall the pain, her breath speeds up. We are back at that moment.

ABI *and* ROSA *on a train platform.* ROSA *is pregnant, seated, concentrating on her breath.* ABI *on her phone.* ROSA *sees her on her phone.*

Is it possible...would you mind if I used your phone? My battery has gone. Is that alright?

ABI Sure.

ROSA Thank you so much.

ABI No problem.

ROSA *makes a call.*

ROSA Mum, it's me. Look, have you got John's number? Well, I'm just on the way to the hospital – no I'm not going into labour, it's just a few pains. I don't know, Mum, I don't know where, where he is, OK. He was out last night, and he's probably tried calling me, but my phone's out of battery, so Mum, can you just get his number for me please? Have you got it? One second *(She begins to tap onto* ABI*'s phone – looks at her apologetically)*

ABI Yeah, go ahead.

ROSA *(she takes down the number)* OK. Thanks, love you.

To ABI, *gesturing to the phone.*

Do you mind?

ABI No.

ROSA Last one, sorry. I really appreciate this. *(On call)* Hello? Who are you? Can you put John on the phone please? Now? John. Who's that? Are you serious, are you actually serious right now? I can't believe you. Do you know what? Don't even – bother.

Hangs up, enraged. Thrusts the phone back to ABI, *who looks sympathetically at her.* ROSA *in a private world of managing pain, anger, and mounting sadness.*

ABI Do you want to use my phone again?

ROSA *shakes her head.*

ROSA Did you hear that?

She's upset, distressed, on her feet now as if willing to walk out of an argument that is in her head.

ABI Maybe you should take a seat.

ROSA I'm going to kill him.

ABI Just breathe.

Pause.

ROSA *(in pain)* Owwwwww. How could he do this?

ABI He's a dick. Let me, let me google, erm. Which hospital?

ROSA Where's the fucking train? St Stephen's.

ABI OK. Fuck.

ROSA Owww.

ABI Look, let's get you a cab. Shall I call one? Have you got cash? I've got cash. *(Fishes out a twenty pound note)*

ROSA You don't need to do that.

ABI Seriously, take it. Come on. You've got a baby in there. Let's get you in a cab.

ROSA *continues to breathe through the pain.* **ABI** *makes a call.*

It's engaged. *(to* **ROSA***)* Fuck it, I'm gonna get you an Uber.

ROSA *has started to cry.*

It's OK, it's OK. Look. Three minutes. Eh? Sorted. Booked. OK. Let's get you to the hospital. The number plate ends with MPV.

ROSA MPV.

ABI Yeah, let's get you to the hospital.

ROSA You don't have to come with me.

ABI No, I won't.

ROSA I'm so sorry. I promise I'll pay you back, I'll give you my email address –

ABI Yep – just put it in there.

ROSA *puts her email into* **ABI***'s phone, breathing through the pain.*

Sent.

ROSA And send me the receipt. *(hands the twenty pound note back)* I won't need this.

ABI You keep it, you might have to pick up some nappies on the way.

ROSA Thank you so much.

ABI It's OK. Good luck. All done, sent.

ROSA *exits.*

ABI, *alone with her phone, and something awfully compelling coming through.*

Scene Seven – Eyewitness accounts

March organisers in the space, almost hesitant, polite.
Speaking directly to TASH.

MO 1 Do you remember me from the rape trial march?

TASH Not really.

MO 1 We met briefly; I was one of the march organisers. I was handing out badges and you said 'Give me a handful, I'll pass them out.'

TASH I can't remember.

MO 2 Should we be going over it like this?

TASH It's OK, you can talk about it. I don't remember it.

MO 1 We did think about having a static rally, but public opinion on the issue was too strong.

MO 2 We didn't want to let the moment pass.

MO 3 We wanted a march.

MO 2 But hadn't organised anything on this scale before.

MO 3 We were a relatively small group.

MO 1 Yeah. / Not that that was.

MO 3 Now we're a bigger group.

MO 2 We were told to keep the route simple. Point A to Point B. / The police were really keen to.

MO 1 Minimum road closures, y'see.

MO 2 Yeah. Keep as many roads open as possible. Mackay Square was the destination.

MO 1 Look, maybe we should –

TASH It's fine.

Shift – the space begins to build with witnesses.

VOLUNTEER I was volunteering as a steward because I wanted to do more than march. The first people I saw turn up, they had glitter on their faces. Maybe they hadn't been home or something from a night out, but I saw these shiny twinkling faces and I thought – yeah. It's going to be a good day.

MO 2 A good atmosphere.

MO 3 A lot of anger and upset had prompted the march, but we wanted it to be positive.

MO 1 We had a briefing with the stewards first thing.

MO 3 And it was a much bigger turnout than expected.

FATHER I was with my daughter, who is only five. I'd got a message from a friend and she said 'There's quite a big group of us going, lots bringing kids, bring Ava with you, it'll be fun.' So I did.

ENTHUSIASTIC PROTESTOR It was just a really good atmosphere, like. It was, you know when you have all this pent up aggro in you and you want to go like 'rahhhhh', let it all out, but then you get together with all these strangers, and it like, it like comes out as love. Like really loving. Because you're like, I can't actually be angry with anyone here.

RELUCTANT FRIEND I wasn't gonna go but my mates dragged me, I was so fucking hungover. My mate said we're only marching from here to the square, once 'we're done we'll go for a Maccy's.'

MO 1 I was at the starting point, essentially at the front of the march.

MO 2 I was with a bunch of volunteers.

MO 3 It was my job to hold back, with the final wave of protestors, at the tail end.

ENTHUSIASTIC PROTESTOR I saw a little girl with a tutu on her head with an A4 sign that said 'There is womb for improvement.' Made me laugh.

COSTA ONLOOKER I was sitting by the window in Costa, in Mackay Square, I was meant to be revising. I didn't know about the march, but I could see all the stalls and stuff out on the square.

FATHER People holding hands and chanting.

VOLUNTEER Having some banter with people.

FATHER I put Ava on my shoulders.

MO 1 All going to plan, until we reached the Square.

VOLUNTEER On Mackay Square, just past the library.

COSTA ONLOOKER It was full of protestors at this point.

MO 3 At the back we'd almost reached the Square.

MO 1 We stop at the stage area, where the first speaker was due to be on.

VOLUNTEER And then suddenly.

RELUCTANT FRIEND A car.

VOLUNTEER Coming towards the square.

COSTA ONLOOKER Fast.

VOLUNTEER What's he doing?

COSTA ONLOOKER Really fast.

VOLUNTEER Not braking.

MO 2 Not going to stop.

COSTA ONLOOKER Slams straight into the crowd.

RELUCTANT FRIEND Into protestors.

MO 2 People go flying.

COSTA ONLOOKER Right up in the air.

RELUCTANT FRIEND Like nothing I've ever seen.

MO 2 Hitting the bonnet of the car and the sound.

VOLUNTEER Like a crunch.

MO 2 It smashes into the Women's Aid stall.

COSTA ONLOOKER Under the wheel of the car.

VOLUNTEER There's someone under the wheel of the car, a girl, a woman, I can't see her face but her bag, which is wedged right under the tyre, totally flattened, and her arm is at a really strange angle.

COSTA ONLOOKER Awful.

MO 2 And then.

VOLUNTEER Panic.

MO 3 Screaming.

MO 2 Panic.

MO 1 Absolute pandemonium.

ENTHUSIASTIC PROTESTOR Everyone just 'GO GO GO GO GO.

COSTA ONLOOKER Everyone just fucking RAN.

MO 3 Chaos, absolute chaos, no one knowing what to do.

FATHER Commotion.

MO 3 The screaming, I've never heard anything like it.

FATHER Gripped onto Ava and ran.

RELUCTANT FRIEND Total chaos.

ENTHUSIASTIC PROTESTOR Like people just falling over.

FATHER I was knocked over, someone trampled on top of us. Stamped on Ava's hand. Broke it.

MO 3 Horrific – bodies on the ground, and so much blood.

MO 1 People crying.

ENTHUSIASTIC PROTESTOR We didn't know if we were running into danger, like it's a –

MO 1 Terrorist thing.

MO 3 Or a bomb.

ENTHUSIASTIC PROTESTOR Everyone just panicking.

RELUCTANT FRIEND A car, it was a fucking car.

FATHER Ava just screaming in pain.

COSTA ONLOOKER I can't believe I'm seeing this.

RELUCTANT FRIEND Literally physically sick.

ENTHUSIASTIC PROTESTOR Just blood everywhere.

COSTA ONLOOKER Please let this be an accident. But you know it isn't.

MO 2 The guy gets out of the car. The driver, he was young.

MO 1 Ross Barton, he gets out of the car, and he's running away from the Square.

VOLUNTEER I started chasing him, I think out of adrenaline.

RELUCTANT FRIEND I saw this steward running towards him.

VOLUNTEER Just sort of threw myself at him.

COSTA ONLOOKER The workers at Costa locked the door and told us that we were not allowed to leave.

MO 1 He's on the floor.

VOLUNTEER He kicked me. Cracked my ribs.

RELUCTANT FRIEND Just trying to call my mum and tell her, but she wouldn't answer, so I kept calling to say.

ENTHUSIASTIC PROTESTOR I'm safe.

ABI I'm safe.

MO 3 I'm safe.

RELUCTANT FRIEND When I finally got through, she's like 'What do you mean –'

FATHER You're safe?

RELUCTANT FRIEND And I'm like, 'Turn on the fucking news!'

COSTA ONLOOKER A policeman.

VOLUNTEER An on-duty copper.

MO 1 Gets to him, pins him down, arrests him.

RELUCTANT FRIEND Nah Mum, someone drove, just drove into the crowd – yeah like fully drove full speed into the crowd – I know! It's fucked!

MO 2 The poor girl. Under the car.

ABI *sits at her laptop.*

ABI When I left the house on that mild Saturday morning my main thought was 'I should have brought a coat.' That was my main concern. My friend Tash had messaged me to say that she was waiting for me outside the court. But when I got there, the march had already started, so I moved through the crowd to try and find her. I turned onto Mackay Square, and I could see her. I called to her, and she turned around, waved at me. She was smiling. Seconds later the car drove into the crowd and hit her. It is a sight I will never forget. I'm in shock. I'm scared. But I find myself asking: what do we do now?

We have to keep the energy of that day burning, especially now, for all of the victims, for Tash, but also for that little girl with the tutu on her head because one day she's going to be twenty one and writing a blogpost and I sure as fuck don't want her to be writing this. I add this blogpost to the thousands of column inches, because I want to mark the change in me that I will never forget.

Everyone engaging with **ABI**'s *blogpost – reading it on their phones.*

Because we're not going to stop talking, and we're not going to stop railing, and we're not going to stop fighting, and we're not going to quit asking people to show up, and stand up, and stand their ground, and we're not going to *stop* each other – we're going to hold each other – and we're going to call it out when we see it, we are going to *name it*:

Their voices chime in with ABI*'s.*

ABI AND MO 3 Hate, the violence, the physical force. Assaults. Attacks.

ABI AND ENTHUSIASTIC PROTESTOR Ross Barton is the latest in a long line.

ABI He won't be the last. Turn these crimes against women, these 'misdemeanours', these masculine 'behaviours' – turn them into crimes directed towards 'children' – you watch the world sit up and protect them. You watch the fury and the disgust and outrage. 'This horrific epidemic we need to stop!'

ABI AND MO 1 AND ENTHUSIASTIC PROTESTOR But we're only women.

ABI AND MO 2 AND VOLUNTEER We don't normalise this bullshit. We don't grow tired and weary of saying 'no' and we aren't going to forget.

ALL We must name it.

ABI I'm writing this blog for my friend, who was at the march on Saturday and is still in Intensive Care.

ALL I'm writing this for you Tash McKendrick.

ABI Because I want to write your name.

ALL Tash McKendrick.

ABI Don't whisper it.

ALL Name it.

Scene Eight – Fast forward Abi's rise

COOKIE *and co, relaying to* TASH.

COOKIE I messaged Abi to find out where she was, but in all the commotion, we didn't see her until the next day. I knew she was OK because she'd marked herself as safe, but it wasn't until the next day when I read the blogpost that I found out what happened.

SEB She came round to my house. She was upset. She asked if she could borrow my laptop.

COOKIE She hadn't written anything like that before.

TOLU It was normally a lifestyle blog, wasn't it?

TOBIAS I was numb at the time, but I read the blog and I'm not embarrassed, I cried.

TOLU I didn't think it was ever going to matter.

WILL Go on, Abi! Make it heard! I didn't know she was a writer, man?!

SEB Since then I'm always like – that blog? She wrote it on *my* laptop.

COOKIE Lots of requests from journalists, and Abi was someone people could get to.

TOBIAS Then there was the vlog not long after, the one of you in the hospital bed.

TOLU I didn't agree with it.

TASH It's fine.

TOBIAS We did get permission from your family.

TASH Honestly.

SEB I'm not really a hashtag person, so I didn't see it coming.

COOKIE For the vigil she wanted to re-read the blog, and I was like, yes, it's strong. You should do it.

SEB Watching the news and it came on – Abi being Abi, on the fucking telly.

WILL Yo, come here man!

Cut to –.

RADIO PRESENTER 1 Abi, you've been an activist at the centre of the movement that grew out of the Mackay Square attack.

ABI Yes, it's had a huge impact on me, it was a traumatic experience.

RADIO PRESENTER 1 Has it been difficult for you to activate, as it were, when you have a friend who is still in a critical condition?

ABI No, it's made it easier actually. It's what's driving me.

Cut to –.

BYSTANDER Are you...? Are you the girl...?

ABI Abi.

BYSTANDER Yeah, I thought it was. I just wanted to say thanks. I was at the march that day and your words at the vigil, they really meant a lot.

ABI Oh thanks. How are you doing?

BYSTANDER I don't know. Can I have a hug?

ABI Erm. Yeah.

Cut to –.

JOURNALIST Why did you write it?

ABI It was important for me to put into words what I'd seen that day because I don't want to become a voiceless, faceless bystander, y'know, we're not just a collective of 'victims' – I don't want us to be seen as victims.

JOURNALIST But you are victims.

ABI We're more than that. We were only at Mackay Square to call out an injustice that we felt strongly about, and for the day to end in tragedy, in the way that it did – that is a staggering example of what we are talking about.

Cut to –.

PUBLICIST That was great! You were great!

ABI Really?

PUBLICIST Yes, brilliant, it's just been picked up by the Beeb. Just keep an eye on – y'know, avoid being confrontational.

ABI Was that confrontational?

PUBLICIST No, no it was fine. I've had two interview requests come in but I'm not sure either of them are right.

ABI Right?

PUBLICIST Right profile.

ABI OK.

PUBLICIST You've got 68,000 followers! I'm holding out for the Guardian.

Cut to –.

ABI Are you at the hospital?

COOKIE On my way.

ABI Any news?

COOKIE Just the same.

ABI OK.

COOKIE We're going to Tash's mums on Sunday.

ABI Yeah, I know, I'm gonna try and make it. Did she mention the foundation idea?

COOKIE Yes.

ABI I just think we need to find a way we can raise money, like properly.

COOKIE Agreed.

Cut to –.

MARCH ORGANISER 1 Brilliant idea.

ABI I thought so.

MARCH ORGANISER 1 We want to put a statement out, so look, maybe we'll send it to you and you can cast your eye over it.

ABI Yep sure thing.

MARCH ORGANISER 1 I can't believe this is happening.

ABI I know.

MARCH ORGANISER 1 I can't get over it. I can't sleep.

ABI Have you got someone to talk to?

MARCH ORGANISER 1 Oh yeah I'll be fine.

ABI You will be.

MARCH ORGANISER 1 Pulling together now is the only way to get through it.

ABI Agreed.

Cut to –.

RADIO PRESENTER 1 So, Incel.

ABI Yes.

RADIO PRESENTER It stands for 'Involuntary Celibate'.

ABI I know what it stands for; Ross Barton had direct links to the Incel movement.

RADIO PRESENTER 1 Allegedly.

ABI He'd posted comments about using violent acts against women because they wouldn't 'put out'.

RADIO PRESENTER 1 But this wasn't solely –

ABI It's not an accident that he targeted that march in particular. That is an act of terror, directed at female protesters.

RADIO PRESENTER 1 There were male protestors present, which is my point; your theory about the Incel movement doesn't quite stack up.

ABI This isn't 'theory' anymore! This is real. This is what happens when you don't challenge misogyny, it goes on and on and on until someone drives a car into you.

Cut to –.

DAISY *(on skype)* Hi Abi!

JOANNA Hi!! Where are you?

DAISY We miss you!

JOANNA Daisy is being asked if YOU are THE Abi.

DAISY Yeah, everyone at school is obsessed with you! #NameIt. I'm gonna get it tattooed, Abs.

JOANNA No she's not. When can we see you?

ABI I don't know, guys, it's all a bit crazy.

JOANNA Are you OK?

ABI I don't know! Hang on, sorry there's a call coming through –

Cut to –.

PUBLICIST Now – just to warn you – this stuff does tend to attract people with their own agendas and vendettas. Any skeletons in the closet?

ABI What do you mean?

PUBLICIST Anyone got anything on you? Ex-boyfriend with naked selfies.

ABI Oh, too many to count.

PUBLICIST Excellent. *(Checks phone)* You've been verified! You're almost at 100,000 followers!

Cut to -.

RADIO PRESENTER 1 Are you presuming to speak for all women?

ABI No.

RADIO PRESENTER 1 Well you're certainly presenting yourself –

ABI No. I'm just a woman. Who is speaking.

RADIO PRESENTER 1 The hash tag #NameIt – you coined it.

ABI Yeah. I just want to encourage women to name what they see. That's directly inspired by Tash, I know she was passionate about this issue. I want to name it, even now – I'm being interviewed by a man – were there no female presenters for this slot?

RADIO PRESENTER 1 Let's go to the news...

Cut to -.

JOURNALIST Your interview with Piers Morgan.

ABI Yes, that was interesting.

JOURNALIST Do you regret it?

ABI I regret everything Piers Morgan says.

JOURNALIST It went viral.

ABI I think Piers Morgan has enough airtime as it is, maybe we can focus on what I'm here to talk about.

Cut to -.

HEADTEACHER Welcome! They're all ready and very excited!

ABI What's the project?

HEADTEACHER Year seven doing Inspirational Leaders.

ABI I take it you haven't told them I got suspended for selling weed.

HEADTEACHER No, we'll steer away from that I think. Have you got your speech prepped?

ABI What speech?

HEADTEACHER You're going to be great.

Cut to –.

DOC FILM MAKER Why you, Abi?

ABI Do you mean, getting this attention? Look, I didn't set out to be an activitist. Activitist? Is that – sorry – can we do that again?

DOC FILM MAKER Rolling. Why you, Abi?

ABI I didn't set out to be an activist, I'm just someone experiencing this stuff in the world and people are responding to that authenticity I suppose.

Cut to –.

TOBIAS *(on the phone)* Mate, call me back, forgetting what you look like – oh no I'm not, because you're ON THE FRONT OF FUCKING STYLIST MAGAZINE.

Cut to –.

ABI *and* **SEB** *hugging hello.*

FAN Excuse me, sorry. Can I get a selfie with you?

ABI Erm, well I'm just in the middle of something –

SEB No, no no. Go for it.

ABI Well.

SEB She's all yours.

FAN #NameIt! *(Snaps)* Thanks!

Scene Nine – Abi's late for Sunday lunch

SEB, **JOANNA** *and* **DAISY** *killing time whilst a roast chicken slowly cools in the kitchen. Slightly awkward and stilted.*

SEB I know she was really looking forward to it.

JOANNA And it's nice we get to hang out.

SEB Yeah.

JOANNA 'Cause I feel like I've only met you in passing.

SEB Well you have.

JOANNA Yeah.

SEB Yeah. She said you guys were going to be doing some filming?

JOANNA Us?

DAISY What?

SEB I think so.

ABI *enters.*

JOANNA Abi, fuck's sake!

ABI I'm sorry!

DAISY *off to get the food.* **ABI** *calling after her.*

Daze...?

JOANNA She's fine. She cooked.

ABI I'm so sorry, I got waylaid. Hey babe.

JOANNA *off stage getting more plates and wine.*

SEB Did it go OK?

ABI Yeah it did, but...

SEB What?

ABI Something has come up.

SEB What d'you mean?

ABI We can't really stay.

SEB What?

ABI I know, it's just they really want me to go to this thing.

SEB Let's just eat. I think she's gone to a lot of effort.

ABI It's just fucking lunch.

> **DAISY** and **JOANNA** *have entered and overheard.*

DAISY It's actually a roast chicken. And I'm trying to be a vegan. And you know that.

ABI That is so kind. Thank you, Daisy.

JOANNA Let's eat!

ABI Guys, this is really awkward, but I'm just going to – there's a thing I have to go to tonight.

DAISY When?

ABI Now.

JOANNA Abi.

ABI It's the film crew, they need some content. There's an event and they managed to get me a ticket. Us a ticket. I got a plus one. I've got a cab outside waiting.

DAISY Are you for real?

ABI It's a networking thing / I know it's a pain.

> **DAISY** *complaining to* **JOANNA** *under her breath.*

DAISY I can't believe this.

JOANNA I know, it's not ideal.

ABI They need to get footage of me for the documentary *(twigs* **DAISY** *and* **JOANNA** *are complaining).* Guys do you want to wait for me to leave before you start bitching.

DAISY I'm not bitching, I'm just saying.

ABI Daisy, I'm sorry, but I have got so much going on right now – and I could really do with your support.

DAISY You've got a lot on? I've got my A-Levels and the Duke of Edinburgh –

JOANNA Guys – look, if you need to go, Abi.

ABI Only because of the film crew. I'd much rather stay here.

DAISY Oh yeah, right. We've marked this date for like seven years now, and Mum and Dad would be so annoyed with you if they knew that you were –

ABI If Mum and Dad were here they'd be really proud of me actually.

SEB Look just go, I'll stay.

ABI No, I begged to get you a ticket!

DAISY I'll have his ticket.

ABI Sorry, Daze, they want Seb.

DAISY Have fun then!

ABI But they do want to film us though, all together, talking about Mum and Dad and how we've all managed –

DAISY Woah.

JOANNA Why do they want to know about that?

ABI Not in detail, just the general.

DAISY Fuck's sake.

JOANNA I don't think I want to do that.

ABI OK, it's just something they mentioned. No. Look. It's fine. Don't worry, we need to go. Come on. I've got people depending on me and pulling me this way and that, y'know –

JOANNA I get it, I get it.

ABI *(to both)* If it was you I would support you.

DAISY Cab's waiting!

Scene Ten – Boyfriend bliss

ABI and SEB in a perfectly sealed world of contentment, focused and wordless watching a film. Their hands stray to each other, always touching, always connected.

SEB   Amongst all the madness there were moments when the world outside gave us breath.

ABI   *(not looking at him)* I think you're beautifu, Seb.

SEB   When I got to watch her just be quiet.

A shift, his bedroom, ABI forensically looking at his clothes in the wardrobe.

I got a free pass wherever she went, which was a buzz.

ABI   Try this.

SEB   But if we had to go to one of her events she would not agree on anything I was wearing. She was bombarding me with clothes and I barely managed to get one top on before –

ABI   No, it's not working. Try this *(tosses him something else)*.

SEB   And she'd be back digging through my wardrobe until –

ABI   Wrong colour. Try this *(tosses something else)*.

SEB   We finally landed on –

ABI   Or maybe that one.

SEB   Which I think is what I had on originally.

ABI   Perfect.

They shift into observing, standing at Ally Pally looking out over London.

SEB   She took me to places I'd never been before.

ABI   How've you never been up here?

SEB   I don't know, it's cool, all the lights, all those people.

ABI Like a constellation. A human one.

SEB Is this where you bring all your boys, then?

ABI Every single one, yeah. Actually, it's where I used to come with Tash.

SEB I like it.

ABI It's beautiful, but it's almost too much. Do you ever feel like you want to plug out, just...disconnect from it all, like – as much as you wanna be part of it, you also want to not be. That's not a depressing thing, it's just, I think that's natural. Does that make any sense?

SEB I think so.

ABI Yeah.

They spin back onto the couch, but in a different seated position, a different film, a different time.

SEB I don't think it was an easy time for her, she was working too hard, not sleeping enough.

Cut to –.

ABI*'s phone pings.*

Seriously, Abs, it's three am.

ABI I know, sorry.

SEB Who is it?

ABI It's nothing.

SEB Plus she was starting to get a bit of stick online, but she didn't like to talk about it.

ABI *on her phone, looking stricken.* **SEB** *grabs it off her.*

No emails tonight.

ABI *(panicked)* Seb! Give that back now. I'm not joking.

SEB I felt like my job was to distract her from it. *(To* **ABI***)* I'll give it you back on the condition you turn it off. Unplug, remember?

ABI OK.

SEB Promise?

She nods. He hands it over.

ABI I love you.

Beat.

SEB This is the first time you ever said it.

ABI I know.

SEB I love you too.

Scene Eleven – Hospital scene

TASH's *hospital room,* TOLU, COOKIE *and* TOBIAS *are all there.* TOBIAS *is painting* TASH's *nails;* COOKIE *is clumsily trying to arrange some flowers in a vase in a way that suggests she doesn't really care.* TOLU *is reading a shit mag. It's quiet.*

ABI *enters.*

ABI Hi guys.

They all greet her, softly but pleased to see her.

TOBIAS Hey, superstar.

ABI Hey.

COOKIE *hugs her, it's quiet but genuine. They speak in hushed tones, almost out of respect for* TASH, *and not to draw too much attention to the number of them in the room.*

TOBIAS You wanna sit?

ABI No, no no.

TOLU I'm not sure how many of us can be in here.

ABI OK, shall I wait?

COOKIE It's fine, I'm heading now.

Pause.

ABI How you doing, Tash?

Pause.

I went into the wrong room by accident.

TOLU They moved her last week.

ABI How is she?

COOKIE She's good.

ABI Yeah?

TOBIAS Might be able to take her off the respirator.

ABI Oh wow.

COOKIE Yeah.

They look at **TASH**.

ABI Doing good, girl.

Pause.

TOLU How are you?

ABI Not bad. Just. Busy.

TOLU Yeah.

Pause.

ABI How's the flat?

TOLU Got a new flatmate... *(Gestures to* **COOKIE***)*

ABI Oh.

COOKIE Yeah.

ABI Amazing.

COOKIE The dream team.

ABI Did – you – who moved out?

COOKIE You did.

TOLU Will did.

Pause.

ABI Yeah, sorry guys. I know. Just. Staying at Seb's. Bit easier.

TOBIAS I was going to ask, my sister is coming to stay next week and I was thinking, if you're not going to be in.

ABI Yeah, of course...

TOBIAS I was going to message you to ask.

ABI No fine, fine, use my room, yeah.

Pause.

Nice nails, Tobes.

Pause.

TOLU Anyone want water?

ABI No thanks.

TOLU *exits. Silence.* **ABI**'s *phone goes off.*

COOKIE No phones, babe.

ABI Yeah. I thought I turned it off but. *(Switches it off)*

Pause.

COOKIE You up to much?

ABI Erm, yeah, I've got a – like there's, someone has dropped out of a talk thing, so I'm filling in. I've got to do a speech.

COOKIE Cool.

ABI At the WoW Festival?

COOKIE Women of the World?

ABI Yeah.

COOKIE That's amazing. We. We went last year. Me and Tash.

ABI Yeah? I'm just filling in.

COOKIE Still. Like. That's a thing.

TOBIAS *(chants, but quietly)* Abi! Abi! Abi!

COOKIE Have you written it yet?

ABI Kind of.

Pause.

TOBIAS Do you remember that Stacey from the BBQ?

ABI How could I forget Stacey?

COOKIE "Are you personally invested?"

TOBIAS She's dating Will now.

ABI What about Tolu?

TOBIAS Broke up with him.

ABI Shit.

COOKIE She was a tit.

> *Pause.*

> So. Can we come and see your speech?

ABI I think so. I don't know.

COOKIE Is it just you?

ABI Hmm.

COOKIE Can you get us tickets?

ABI I can absolutely get you a ticket.

TOBIAS And me?

ABI I will definitely try and remember, yes.

TOBIAS A flat outing.

ABI Cool.

COOKIE That's great, Abi.

> *Pause.*

> Look, if you want to send me a draft, I'm happy to help with it.

ABI Oh no, I'll be fine.

> **TOLU** *returns.*

TOLU Guys, we can't all be in here.

TOBIAS OK, I'm off.

COOKIE Yeah, I'm going to head.

ABI I'm going to stay a bit.

As **TOBIAS** *gets up to leave* **ABI** *takes his seat and takes* **TASH***'s hand.*

TOBIAS Don't smudge them!

ABI Sorry. *(Lets go)*

TOLU Come and see us, yeah?

ABI I will, I will.

TOBIAS See ya, Abi.

COOKIE Bye, Abi. Bye Tash.

ABI Bye, guys.

They leave. **COOKIE** *hangs back, watching her.*

Love you.

Alone with **TASH.**

Hi, Tashtash, how you doing? I'm sure everyone has been keeping you updated. Things with me are crazy. Just. Intense. I'm not... I'm fine. But. It's. We miss you. All the time.

I think I need your help with this. *(Brings out her speech)*

So. They said open brief. Which is actually harder. Something uplifting to end the day. OK.

Thanks very much, thank you, Jude. It's a real privilege to be here today with you all, even as a substitute for who you really wanted to see. I'm thrilled to stand in.

For the last six months I feel I've been standing in for someone very, very important to me, so it's a role that comes easily. You may have heard me mention Tash McKendrick's name, or you may have read it, or maybe you've even written it.

(to TASH*)* Shall I put in – what do you think? This time last year Tash was in this very room? That's quite nice.

She scribbles out, writes.

Tash was the person who introduced me to the *idea* of women's rights. I naively believed that our rights were like oxygen invisible and constant. I was wrong... I was proven wrong?

(to TASH*)* Is this the right tone? Speak up, babe, I can't hear you.

When we were teenagers in school, taking on the school governors – an entirely male, entirely white group of scintillating individuals – to campaign for girls to be able to wear trousers as part of their uniform, Tash was instrumental.

Pause. COOKIE *has heard enough.*

(To TASH*)* Wake up Tash.

ABI *remains in the space, looking at the bed where* TASH *should be.* TASH *and* COOKIE *watch her, she's in a concealed moment.*

TASH I think I can remember some of this.

COOKIE We thought you might be able to hear us.

TASH Some of the things that she just said –

COOKIE Yeah?

TASH The speech. That feels...familiar.

COOKIE But you know that story about the school trousers.

TASH Yeah, suppose.

Pause.

Abi?

She doesn't respond.

Scene Twelve – Rosa confronts Abi

The Southbank Centre is bright and buzzing. **ABI** *glancing at her notes and muttering to herself, prepping herself to be proper WOW.* **ROSA** *approaches her, with a pram, tries to meet her eyes.*

ROSA Abi?

ABI Hi.

ROSA You don't recognise me, do you? I've seen you on TV, y'see.

ABI Oh.

ROSA But you don't...

ABI Sorry.

> *Pause.*

I'm Abi.

ROSA I know. I'm Rosa.

ABI Hi, I'm really sorry –

ROSA I've been / trying to –

ABI I'm really sorry I'm just – sorry!

ROSA No it's –

ABI I'm just practising; I could do with. Just. I don't want to be rude.

ROSA I emailed you.

ABI Oh.

ROSA You didn't respond.

ABI Oh. Maybe it went into my junk.

ROSA A few times. You don't remember me?

ABI Not sure.

ROSA You helped me, at the train station. The day of the attack.

Penny drops for ABI.

ABI Oh yeah. You were. Yes. *(Pointing)* The baby!

ROSA Yeah, Emily, this is Emily. *(They peer at her)* She's asleep.

ABI How you doing?

ROSA Good thanks, yeah. She's, it's been intense. But yeah.

ABI Good. I'm sorry, but I need to get / get going.

ROSA I owe you money.

ABI No you don't.

ROSA Twenty quid.

ABI It's fine. Keep it. You probably need it.

Pause.

ROSA I don't need it.

ABI *reluctantly takes.*

ABI Well. We're square. You really shouldn't have come all this way for twenty quid.

ABI *goes to leave –* PUBLICIST *approaches.*

PUBLICIST That's five minutes, Abi.

ABI OK fine.

PUBLICIST Do you want a glass of water?

ABI Yes please.

PUBLICIST I'll pop it on the stage. *(To* ROSA*)* Hi.

ROSA Hi.

PUBLICIST I think they're going in now, if you want to take a seat.

PUBLICIST *leaves.*

ROSA I've been following you and everything, I think what you're doing is great.

ABI Well, it's not just me.

ROSA Seriously.

ABI Well thank you, that's kind, but I've got to go.

ROSA But something has been niggling me.

Pause.

The morning of the attack. You weren't at the protest.

Pause.

ABI I was.

ROSA You weren't. You were with me.

Pause.

ABI I was there.

ROSA You couldn't have got to Mackay Square –

ABI I did.

ROSA Abi. I've got the Uber receipt. With the time on. The car attack happened five minutes before that. It's not possible that you were there, you couldn't have got there.

ABI I'm sorry – what is this?

ROSA I'm not being / I'm just –

ABI Are you trying to – hang on a minute –

ROSA Because I think / what you've been doing –

ABI No, excuse me –

ROSA Is, is –

ABI Are you? Is this? What?

ROSA I wanted to give you the money back and –

ABI Have a go at me!

ROSA Ask you / no, not having a go –

ABI I can't believe this. Haven't you got more important things to be doing than coming here and – what?

ROSA I just wanted to talk to you.

ABI Haven't you got enough to focus on? *(Gesturing to baby)*

ROSA Excuse me?

ABI The media manipulate things all the time, y'know, you say something and they take it out of context, / they change what you say.

ROSA No, hang on. I see you on TV, and in the paper, and everything you preach is about being honest, about naming it.

Pause.

But you've been lying this whole time, haven't you?

ABI Can you keep your voice down.

ROSA All this time.

ABI What exactly –

ROSA You were saying / you were there and you went through this trauma.

ABI What exactly do you think I'm lying about? Do you think I'm lying about the issue? About what's at stake?

ROSA No –

ABI That women's rights aren't / important?

ROSA Don't patronise me.

ABI That we don't need –

ROSA I'm not saying that.

ABI What?

ROSA I'm saying that you weren't there and you're profiting off it.

ABI Profiting?

ROSA Yes. Am I the only one that knows?

ABI You know what we should be talking about, we should be talking about that man, about Ross Barton, who drove the car into us, / who injured innocent people –

ROSA Please don't shout, he didn't drive a car into you, Abi.

ABI We should be talking about that.

ROSA That whole protest that day was / about proving that women –

ABI Not – I'm not the villain.

ROSA Don't lie about these situations, and here you are – lying.

ABI Do you think I'm doing this for myself? I'm not, I'm doing it for everyone. I'm a force for change, I'm trying to do some good and who the fuck are you?

Pause.

ROSA I'm a mum. Raising her daughter in an honest home.

ABI I'm fighting for the right that you aren't questioned for being a stay-at-home-mum? OK?

ROSA I'm sorry? / You're doing what??

ABI I'm fighting for your daughter, and her daughters! / You don't get it, do you?

ROSA Oh, how noble of you!

ABI You just don't get it.

ROSA Oh, you've got a really over-inflated / sense of yourself, haven't you.

ABI Look. I've got. I've got a speech to do, OK? That's what I'm doing here. What are you doing? Harassing me. So why don't you just fuck off.

Pause.

ROSA So much for solidarity, eh Abi?

ABI I'm doing more than you are.

ROSA I bet a lot of people are coming to see you today.

ABI Yeah.

ROSA And you're taking the piss out of them and what they stand for.

ABI I'm not!

ROSA They ought to know.

ABI What – are you going to tell them?

> ABI *turns on her heel – instantly it shifts to the end of her speech, her speech notes quivering in her hand. She's smiling, but deep down a low tide of unease. Applause begins slowly, but builds – she's nailed the speech. Someone approaches her hand, shakes it, a photo is snapped. Someone else congratulates her.* ABI *breathes through it, ever the professional.*

Scene Thirteen – Abi confides in Seb

ABI *and* SEB *together – he can see she's flustered.*

SEB Look, calm down –

ABI But.

SEB Come here.

ABI Seb –

SEB It's been a big week.

ABI Will you just listen –

SEB And you've been stressed out, and it was a big deal tonight, and the adrenalin is pumping.

ABI Yeah, but she ambushed me before the speech and she said all this stuff and I was just, I was so nervous / my mind just –

SEB Don't take any notice of some idiot, she's probably just jealous, or she couldn't get a ticket, or I don't know – she's – ignore her. Don't let it take the shine off your night!

Pause.

You know when you do stuff like this the crazies come crawling out. You've got to bat them off, Abi. You want to see the response it got – have you seen? So much love for you out there, and love for Tash, and – ah man – I'm so proud of you, y'know. C'mon.

What?

Pause.

ABI She thinks I was never at the march.

SEB What – Mackay?

ABI Yeah.

SEB But you were.

ABI Yeah.

SEB So fuck her.

ABI Yeah.

SEB That's – some people, man. She probably just wants to *be* you – that's her problem.

ABI It really upset me.

SEB I bet it did. Come here. You know what you need, don't you? A pint of champagne.

SEB *picks her up, hoists her like a fireman's lift – she is shocked into squealing – she wants to remain inconspicuous.*

ABI No –

SEB Yes you do, my treat, come on.

ABI Seb, I just want to go home.

SEB There's going to be an after-party here with your name on.

ABI Seb! Put me down!

SEB Now ,I'm sure I saw a bar round here –

ABI Seb, please!

SEB *is playful, trying to cajole her out of herself.* ABI, *protesting at first, begins to laugh as he gets more outlandish, spinning her round.*

SEB Now this will be easier if you don't struggle.

ABI SEB!!!

It builds to a small crescendo – it's frenetic and fun – until he gives in and places her down. They are out of breath, smiling, looking at each other with laughter.

Just the sound of their breath. ABI *watches him.*

SEB Two days later, the story broke.

A handful of tweets – initial reactions – burst into life.

– Wtf?? Can't believe what I am reading this morning #NameIt exposed

– So disappointed in Abi Spiro. Never trust your darlings

– So yep today in shock. You think you know someone... #ImNotwithHer Abi is a / fake

– From every woman in the world, how dare you! Never speak on anyone's behalf again. You need help. @Abi4Change #Nameit / #Fraud #AngryFeminist

– always wondered if abi spiro was full of shit / looool

– @abi4change i wish i had that sorta time

Scene Fourteen – Journo and paparazzi

The JOURNALIST, RADIO PRESENTER 1, PUBLICIST *and* PAPARAZZI *onstage.*

JOURNALIST Look, I'm not going to lie, I wasn't exactly skipping to the editor when this came to me. It's a shame for the girl, I mean, I like the girl, but I've got a job to do and when she's exposed as a fraud, it's a massive public interest story.

RADIO PRESENTER 1 We'd had Abi on the show a few times and it always kicked off those sort of intense public convos that you live for as a broadcaster.

PAPARAZZI I don't even think *we* realised the amount of attention it would get.

PUBLICIST You're always given a right to reply, if you're the story, and Abi was no different, she had the chance to provide a comment – but she wouldn't speak to me, wouldn't answer my calls. What was I meant to do?

RADIO PRESENTER 1 It was a surprise, because she'd come across as so media savvy. I just assumed she would know how to handle this.

PUBLICIST There's this tiny window when you can impact the story – as much as you ever can – and she let that window slip through her fingers.

JOURNALIST Then – BAM – the story is out and then it's never *not* out. Again. But like I say, I wasn't punching the air.

PAPARAZZI There were seven or eight of us outside the house, waiting, we'd been calling her phone, we'd been calling the house, shouting through the letter box – provoking her to get a reaction. And when she does come out, I'm right there, with my camera ready, and she looks straight down the lens, rookie error – and I've got her – deer in the headlights, not slept for days, no make-up, looking like shit. Couldn't have been better if I'd staged it.

JOURNALIST The worst thing about it was – well, not the worst – it's just a fact, and one you can't necessarily predict when you run a story, but it was a very slow news day.

RADIO PRESENTER 1 All the major agencies picked up on it.

JOURNALIST That's just the luck of the draw, y'know, I can't do anything about that, and my tone was very, very reserved. It was the facts.

RADIO PRESENTER We ran a phone-in on the day it broke – I couldn't believe the response.

JOURNALIST Abi was a poster girl, and it was a slow news day. And sometimes circumstances collide to make the most fertile breeding ground for a story ever.

PAPARAZZI 'The downfall of an untouchable feminist darling', and she's looking like a bag lady and I'm thinking – kerching!

RADIO PRESENTER 1 Yes, it's a shame. But she made her bed.

More tweets float in from the ether:

– @Abi4Change you have driven a metaphorical car into the feminist movement / #RossBartonLookALike

– fuck drake i wanna hear Pusha T diss this / abi bitch

– Lol bitch is dismantling feminism everywhere. Go Abi. Yeah fucking #NameIt / #Whore

– I just rewatched one of @abiforchange interviews with ITV news. She literally says / "I am a liar and I suck Dicks for breakfast"

– ok @abi4change ill #NameIt. Women like you are the reason women stay silent. Women like you are why the word of abuse survivors is not trusted. Women like you are why men like Mark Rendell / get acquitted.

– @abiforchange is so problematic, I could see straight through her the moment she wore a jean jacket with Crocs. Dafuq

– She's a liar but who cares I'd still tap that xx @Abi4Change

Scene Fifteen – Seb confronts Abi

ABI *and* SEB, *mid-flight in a downward spiral. He's torn – wanting to protect her, question her, absolve her.*

SEB   What the fuck –

ABI   Please.

SEB   Is there something wrong with you?

ABI   I know, but you said –

SEB   You stood there and you said you was at the march –

ABI   I was trying to protect you!

SEB   Don't worry about me! You need to look after yourself.

ABI   I've got to do something, I've got to draft something / or I should –

SEB   That's the least of your worries.

ABI   I need your help / I just –

SEB   What am I going to –

ABI   I just need to sit and go through everything.

SEB   They're not being kind, Abi.

ABI   I know!

SEB   If I were you I would just keep your head down –

ABI   I can't, I've got to, I'm getting, like everyone is on my back / and I've got to be able to stick up –

SEB   You should leave it!

ABI   For myself. Seb! It's on the front page.

SEB   I know! / And whose fucking fault is that?

ABI   How am I meant to leave it?? Please can you just stop shouting.

SEB   What did you expect was going to happen?!

ABI Please! I need your help!

Pause.

Should I go to the press?

SEB Honestly?! Just leave it alone.

ABI How?

SEB You've got a lot of support, you've built up this amazing thing. And people admire you.

ABI Yeah but I'm getting / trashed.

SEB You can't do anything about that now!

ABI OK.

SEB Just lay low for a bit. Give it time. It'll blow over.

Gesturing for him.

ABI I love you.

Pause.

SEB It's not like you actually... hurt anyone.

ABI Come here. Please.

He doesn't move.

Tweets tumble together, on top of each other, a discontented cacophony:

– Giving a voice to the voiceless. Wished @Abi4Change had just kept quiet #STFU #NameIt

– @abi4change it makes me cringe that I used to like you.

– The death of a role model

– how do you spell white feminism -A-B-I-S-P-I-R-O

– #NameIt #FeministLiar There's survivor's guilt and then there's this @Abi4Change. Absolutely disgusted.

– I actually respect abi spiro, she stood for something important. Took the pain of this problem and friend in coma to create more awareness. thank you abi

– Abi Spiro has betrayed every little girl across the country who saw hope in her. Name her, shame her.

Scene Sixteen – March organisers deliver statement

March organisers solemnly standing together, delivering a damning eulogy. The press swarms.

MO 1 The news events of the last two days have shocked our small team; we're making this statement today to clear up any misinformation that has been reported.

MO 2 We met Abi Spiro in the aftermath of the Mackay Square attack. We believed, as she had claimed, that she had shared our awful experiences of that day. We had no reason to doubt her; she spoke with passion and insight about her experiences. We were taken in.

MO 3 Her rising profile, both on social media and within the press, has led to her becoming a focal point, and a voice for change. Although we stand by our commitment to fighting gender inequality, we deeply regret our association with Abi Spiro.

MO 1 #NameIt *has* been a positive force. But political movements, such as ours, pre-exist simple hashtag phenomena. We ask our supporters and peers to stand shoulder to shoulder with us at this time, and to overlook the callous and dishonest actions of Abi Spiro.

Overlapping tweets.

– What if we ran her over with a car? Then she wouldn't be lying anymore! Just a feminazi taking up valuable space on the road. #NameIt if you want to be the one to flatten her

– you guys are acting like you weren't loving this abi girl a week ago. But all you woke bitches are still sleeping

– Just had to tell my daughter the truth about Abi. She has just ripped her #NameIt poster in half. I would have done worse

– Can't believe how deluded @Abi4Change was to keep such a lie for so long. That's so ballsy. She's either mentally ill or... nah just mental. (Pic/meme) #picoftheday #abi #NameIt

Scene Seventeen – Abi and siblings

ABI, DAISY and JOANNA – ding-ding, round three. DAISY has a wild animal quality to her, like all the years of rage and angst at being the youngest, being a teenager, losing her parents are simmering over. ABI has been getting it in the neck all day, she is weary and hardened. JOANNA is limp like lettuce, an unwitting referee. There isn't much concession.

DAISY He spat in my food today and called me a 'lying piece of shit'. They all think I knew!

JOANNA I had to leave work early and go and pick her up.

ABI I'm sorry!

DAISY They've all turned on me!

ABI I'm sorry! I'm sorry that you're being bullied by your hideous little friends, OK Daisy, but I can assure you I've had a shitter day than you, OK?!

DAISY What is she even doing here?

JOANNA Calm down, both of you.

DAISY She's fucking barred.

ABI You can't bar me, Daze!?

JOANNA Just shut up! Both of you!

DAISY I don't want her in the house! I don't want to be in the same room as her!

ABI Well get out then! And let the grown-ups talk!

JOANNA Abi, why have you come round here / if you're just going to –

ABI I just need some, / I need to think.

DAISY I'm ACTUALLY ashamed of you.

ABI Great! Great! I'll add you to the list.

JOANNA We can't do this. *(She goes to indicate* **ABI** *should leave)*

ABI *(panicked)* Jo, please.

JOANNA You need to go, Abi.

ABI Please just give me five minutes!

DAISY You heard her.

ABI Shut the fuck up!

JOANNA Don't speak to her like that. Daisy – go and – look, she's in the middle of her UCAS form and it's due in tomorrow and she needs to focus.

ABI I promise I won't stay long.

JOANNA No!

DAISY If you think I'm going to Uni you're out of your fucking mind. Everyone talking there and getting on my back and – how could you do this –

JOANNA Daisy, go to your room.

DAISY You've ruined feminism for everyone!

ABI No I haven't, Daisy, it was there before me and it'll be there after.

DAISY Fuck university, and fuck you. I don't give a shit about my A-Levels. You've ruined my life. I need a cigarette.

JOANNA You don't smoke.

DAISY Yes I do!

ABI Life doesn't start and end with your A-Levels, Daze – and one day you'll realise that when you stop behaving like a fucking CHILD.

DAISY A child?? I didn't get to have a childhood, Abi!, Remember? Oh no you don't, 'cause you ran off as fast as you could out of here, left me with Joanna, left Joanna to take care of me *alone.*

ABI That's not fair.

DAISY You're never here. You got famous off a lie. A fucking lie. Authentic? Fuck off.

JOANNA OK Daze, I know you're upset.

DAISY No, Joanna, she's not the only one who's allowed to call people out, to *Name It*. People are telling the truth about her and she can't handle it –

ABI *(desperate)* No, I can't handle it, I am drowning, Daisy!

JOANNA I'm done with this. *(She goes to leave)*

ABI Jo – please?!

JOANNA You need to leave.

DAISY *(hurling the final dagger)* If Mum was here she would *hate* you. I'm glad she's dead so she doesn't have to see it.

ABI *wounded.*

ABI *(to* JOANNA *– quietly intense)* Are you just going to stand there?

JOANNA *at a loss.*

I really need you / to give me the benefit –

JOANNA So does Daisy. And she didn't ask for any of this.

Pause.

ABI I didn't ask for it, Jo.

JOANNA You need to go.

ABI *walks out.*

Scene Eighteen – Tobias and Tolu

Tweets whispered underneath the scene:

– Abby rose while our sisters fell. We marched against everything she stood for – truth and strength. #feelingsick

– To be honest I inspire to be like @abiforchange. Imagine the months of plotting. Work hard kids and follow your dreams

– #NameIt I spoke out about my experiences because of you Abi. I thought you were on my side. Now I'm naming you as yet another person to have violated my trust

– #Scabby liar @Abby how dare you use a tragedy for your career?! #burninginthelimelight.

TASH   Couldn't you see what was happening to her?

TOLU   Well, we *knew* what was happening, but neither of us had spoken to her. We hadn't seen her for weeks.

TOBIAS   She was standing in the kitchen, you could tell she'd been crying.

TOLU   I did feel a bit like – what are you doing here? All this is kicking off and all of a sudden you're back. I don't know.

TOBIAS   She didn't speak, didn't say anything.

TOLU   I was expecting her to apologise or something. But she didn't.

TOBIAS   She went upstairs to her room and she didn't come out all night.

TOLU   Y'know when you've had a fight with someone and the whole place just feels *awkward??* But we hadn't had a fight! That's what it felt like though. A stand-off.

Scene Nineteen – Seb disowns Abi

SEB, *suddenly back to the last conversation they had. He's loathe to relive it. He asks the other characters.*

SEB She was stood there, right there... Do I have to do this?

TASH I need to hear it.

They don't respond. He's thrust back into that moment.

SEB – *head full of the tweets, the news, the comments, every message* **ABI** *has ever sent him, every message his mother keeps sending him, every single piece of the puzzle is a puncture.*

SEB Every message that you sent me, from that day, and I've been through them.

Pause.

You are so. Convincing.

Pause.

That very day of the march you came back here and you were so distraught.

ABI I was.

SEB So – what *is* that, Abi? Who is that person? Because that person is ill. It's more than just like you faked it for everyone, because you faked it SO WELL, I thought you were this spectacular person, showing off to my mates about you constantly, and trying to be a better person so I could DESERVE you. Do you know what I mean? I was so into you. SO into you. And you've made me look like... You've made it into something flimsy and shit. *That's* the only Abi I know. Isn't it.

ABI Seb –

SEB I don't want an excuse. Have you seen the shit I'm getting? From all sides. And it hasn't got anything to do with me. Have you any idea how humiliating it is to be dragged down to *your* level.

Pause.

I want you to leave.

ABI *almost leaves.*

ABI There's me 'out there', and there's me in here. I know you think they're not the same. But they're not as far away as you think.

SEB I think. They're both fucked.

Tweets vibrating the space:

– Fucking white, pasty ass / no seasoning having ass, fraudulent feminazi lying bitch whore.

In unison:

– @abiforchange looking like an open wound. Let salt bae that bitch.

– Another example of how all women lie #incel #Scabbybitch

– @Abi4Change you narcissistic fucking bitch

– @abi4change you are a disgrace. Such a lowlife piece of shit.

Scene Twenty – Cookie lands the final blow

TASH's hospital room. COOKIE on her phone. A hushed awe when ABI arrives, like no one wants to tread too heavily on the ice, in case it cracks under the weight. COOKIE keeps her focus on TASH, and chooses the moment she wants to skewer ABI by looking at her.

ABI Can I sit down?

COOKIE *doesn't respond.*

COOKIE I won't be in for a few days, Tash, because I'm going away for the weekend, but I'll be back on Tuesday.

ABI Where you off?

COOKIE *quiet.*

Can I come with you?

COOKIE Unbelievable.

ABI You didn't answer my calls.

Pause.

I understand.

Pause.

Cooks. Cookie.

COOKIE I don't think you do. Understand. Because if *you* were watching a woman being crucified for being a fraud – you'd be all over it. You'd love the hysteria, and you'd rant about it on the WhatsApp group, and you'd probably write a bloody blogpost about it. So now that person is – you.

ABI Do you think I meant to hurt you? Really?? Anyone?

COOKIE You said you were physically there! 'It's a sight I will never forget'!? That's fucked up, Abi.

ABI I know.

COOKIE I think you're a fantasist. I think you always want to wedge yourself in the middle of shit. That campaign for school trousers, that was me and Tash. You're a little leach.

Pause. **ABI** *choosing her words carefully.*

ABI I meant every word I said since the attack. I'm trying to work out who I am, and this moment sort of found me and it felt right and I didn't have it in me to stop it. I could've been there, it could have been me in that bed –

COOKIE Don't you dare.

ABI That isn't fantasy. That is just – luck. I'm lucky that I wasn't there.

COOKIE I know! And you're lucky that you look the way you do, Abi, and sound the way you do – and that people sit up and fucking listen when you open *your* mouth. Guess what? I wouldn't have had that opportunity, nor would Tash.

This lands on **ABI**. *She thinks carefully before she speaks.*

ABI You're right. But everything I have done since has been to try and make the most of that luck, and to do the best I can.

COOKIE So fucking manipulative.

ABI I didn't put myself here. Everyone put me here. I wasn't straight, I fully accept that, but I didn't expect any of this to happen.

Silence.

COOKIE I'm just really glad I'm not you. Your name is always going to be associated with this. So – I would just cut the puppy dog shit – and deal with that. Deal with it, Abi. Get on with it. Don't wait for us to let you off the hook. It's not our job.

Tweets spoken, in full, vile voice:

– @abi4change hope someone runs over your family then at least you'll know how it feels.

– One more slut exploiting tragedy for publicity and money. Go back to being a proper whore @Abby

– First one to rape @Abi4change gets lifetime membership to da club #INCEL #lyingslut #NailIt

– #Abi4change you're going to squeal like a fucking pig when we fuck you

– Why don't you just kill yourself?

Scene Twenty One – Abi's online apology

ABI *alone in the space. She is recording her online apology. It isn't easy for her to speak – the struggle between the dignity she aspires to and the pain of what she's lost. Complexity slices through every sentence. At times she's robust, at others she's overcome – back to that teenager who lost her parents and couldn't make sense of the world. A profoundly lonely space, at once hopeless – but the only thing to cling on to. Maybe this will have an impact. Maybe this will matter. Maybe it will bury her further.*

ABI After the Mackay Square march I marked myself as safe on Facebook, because I was safe. I wasn't there when the attack occurred. I had intended to be...but I slept in. The attack happened when I was on my way there, and I later found out that my friend, Tash, had been caught under the vehicle, and I felt so, so guilty that she had waited for me. I couldn't admit that to my friends, so I imagined what could have happened if I had made it there, and I wrote it in a blog, which I thought no one would read except my friends.

That blogpost was the sum total of my fear and rage and anger. It was a fiction, but my feelings were not. I wrote it in the middle of the night, in a moment of private pain – it felt private. That was a grave mistake. When the blogpost got attention, it did me good to have a function. I genuinely believed I could make a difference. Instead that mistake has caused anguish to people I love, many followers who looked up to me. I am truly sorry for the impact of my actions.

For the last two days I have had a torrent of hate levelled at me. Death threats, rape threats, online abuse and intensified news coverage. I accept responsibility for my actions. But it has been difficult to live through.

Please remember that the #NameIt movement came from a place of truth. It doesn't belong to me – it belongs to you. To all of you striving to make the world a better place for women and girls everywhere. It has never been more necessary to raise your voices against hate.

Scene Twenty Two – The community reflect

A space – a gap, ABI's *apology still fresh. Slowly the cast emerge to make sense of what they started. The world stutters – snatched conversations from THEN and moments of clarity NOW.* TASH *is trying really hard to compute it all.*

TOBIAS Guys, did you see this?

SEB A notification on my phone.

WILL I watched it on the bus.

TOLU I watched it at home.

COOKIE I didn't watch it.

DAISY My friend sent me a link.

ROSA Yeah, I saw it.

WILL I sent her a message. 'Lol this is mad, the shade on you. Tune it out. Peace.'

Beat.

TOBIAS Abi. Abi?

TOLU She's not in her room.

JOANNA Not since Tuesday, officer.

SEB No, I haven't heard from her.

JOANNA Do you remember what she was wearing?

DAISY The police wanted a proper description, even though there are tonnes of photos of her online. We still had to describe her.

SEB Abi? Call me back. I'm worried.

WILL If you watch it back –

TOBIAS Don't watch it, Tash.

WILL She looks defeated.

Beat.

TOLU When she was reported missing, it was like waking up with the worst hangover. What did I do last night? You want someone to tell you that you did absolutely nothing wrong.

Beat.

TASH You didn't tell me for weeks.

TOBIAS We couldn't. Doctors' orders.

COOKIE We didn't know what to say, Tash.

An attempt to reach **ABI**.

WILL Abi, you OK?

TOLU Abi, Tash has woken up.

JOANNA Abi, call me back.

Back to **TASH**.

COOKIE Are you OK?

TASH I don't know.

Beat.

What are we doing now?

TOBIAS No one knows.

JOANNA We just wait, wait until she needs us.

TASH We don't know where she is, we don't know if she's...

The **JOURNALIST** *is the first person who wants to grant something like forgiveness – a frankness that cuts through the space.*

JOURNALIST I'm sorry... I didn't expect her to be taken apart like that. Maybe I should have buried it.

DAISY I'm not saying I forgive her, but – because she was, she was wrong, wasn't she? What she did was wrong, wasn't it?

Beat.

That's what we said.

SEB I said things I'm not proud of. But I thought I'd get a chance to take them back.

DAISY We didn't mean it forever, did we?

WILL It's eternal, mate. It's worse than eternal. Because it's on every single screen that's ever been invented.

Beat. A shift in energy – a mixture of attack and defence seeping out. People desperate to have their say.

And it's the sandalled vegans who get me. Animal-loving holy woke executioners, fox-hunting Abi for fun. A lie is a lie is a lie – I get that. But a pearly white lie? Which did some good?

ROSA Do you know what I think? It must be really easy to slip into being someone else. Easy and fun and yeah – must feel like freedom. Who do you want to be today? But that isn't real. It isn't real, but it has real consequences. So there you go. Work harder to be in the real world.

WILL Thank you twitterati. Thank you shittersphere.

*The liminal space of **ABI**'s absence starts to skip – like a record bouncing – stuttering voices and echoes from before, confusing for **TASH**, like she's coming round, a clash of thoughts.*

TOBIAS But, I'm just saying, from the outside, it looked real. It looked like Abi becoming Abi.

MO 1 I think she believed it. Sometimes you get so close to a lie that it becomes you. That's the only way that I can rationalise it.

MO 2 I didn't ever want her to suffer, I just wanted distance, I wanted space – I wanted *her* over *there*.

SEB How did she go from being right here? She was right there.

TOLU When you were out of it, Tash, you weren't there, but you *were* there, y'know? But not being able to get through to her –

TASH Please. Can you stop –

COOKIE I was at your bedside, Tash, and she was at a TV studio. Do you know what I mean?

TASH No, I don't. I don't know what you mean. I wasn't here!

JOANNA Do you remember what she was wearing?

DAISY No, I can't, will you stop asking me?!

TASH Can we go back?

COOKIE We just did, Tash.

TASH But, I mean, to before. Way before.

Suddenly **IGGY** *in the space – a call back.*

IGGY Does anyone want anything for tonight?

TOLU What?

IGGY Because I'm calling him now.

SEB Sun coming up and I'm getting called Kevin and Freddie and Jack.

COOKIE You've got to name that shit. Name it. Remember, Tash?

TOLU You were here, Tash, but you weren't here – do you know what I mean?

MO 2 Should we be going over it like this?

COOKIE Tash.

WILL If you watch the apology back now –

TOBIAS Don't.

WILL She isn't even there.

TASH Stop it! Please.

JOANNA She didn't ask for this.

DAISY We didn't ask for this.

TOBIAS Abi, call me back, I'm forgetting what you look like mate –

TASH Abi? I want to go back.

COOKIE Remember?

TASH No.

TOLU Guys, not being funny, I'm all up for debate but it's my birthday.

COOKIE If you stack up that evidence you've got a really compelling case.

WILL It's over.

COOKIE It is to you.

WILL Jury of public opinion is it?

TASH Stop! I just need a minute. Please. Can I just have a minute on my own?

A reversal of the scene in **TASH***'s hospital room; this time* **TASH** *is talking to an absent* **ABI** *who cannot answer. She is trying to reach her from where she is.*

Abi, it's me. TashTash. I don't know where you are, if you're OK, I don't know if you've done something... You won't answer your phone, babe, can you answer your phone? Remember when we were kids, and we'd spend all day together in school, walk home together, and then call each other as soon as we got through the door, and spend hours talking on the phone? We never ran out of things to say. Let's go back to that.

Beat.

Since I woke up it's like a box set that everyone is obsessed with and you haven't seen it, and then someone says – no, you were IN IT. It's fucked.

Abi?

I read your blogpost. They said not to. But I did. Maybe I should be angry, but I read it and I just wanted to hug you. So if you came back we could talk, we could cry, we could get angry for a bit – but I know we'd be OK. You fucked up. I know. But you didn't drive a car into me.

Abi?

They held you up as a hero, and then you got torn down. All that stuff online about you isn't real to me. Can you hear me? That's not real. Real is you drinking milk and crying it out of your eyes in Year nine, and taking the blame for that weed I brought into school, and staying up with me all night when my Gran died because you said 'if you can't sleep, I can't sleep.'

Abi?

They tore you down. But I want to lift you up, Abi. You're my best friend, we've loved each other a long time.

You're more than the things they said about you.

I hope you can hear me.

Abi?

End

PROPS

Birthday sash
Beer bottles
Tobacco (in a tin or pouch)
Sausage roll
Party cups and straws
Badges with feminist slogans
Mobile phones (for all cast)
Rum and cokes (x 2)
Water bottle
Empty bowl of cereal
Extra Shirts, t-shirts for Seb
Coffees (x3)
Apron
Oven gloves
Nail Varnish
Magazine
Pram
Notebook, with scraps of paper (for speech)
DSLR camera

VISIT THE SAMUEL FRENCH BOOKSHOP AT THE ROYAL COURT THEATRE

Browse plays and theatre books, get expert advice and enjoy a coffee

Samuel French Bookshop
Royal Court Theatre
Sloane Square
London
SW1W 8AS
020 7565 5024

Shop from thousands of titles on our website

 samuelfrench.co.uk

 samuelfrenchltd

 samuel french uk